RUN YOUR OWN POP UP CINEMA
everything you need to know to run your own successful popup cinema business

by Josh Charbon

© 2020 2312 Books
email: books@2312.uk

No part of this publication may be reproduced, distributed, stored in or introduced into a retrieval system or transmitted in any way without the written permission of the Copyright Holder.

© 2312 Books
- April 1, 2020 -

LIMIT OF LIABILITY/DISCLAIMER OF WARRANTY

The publisher and author make no representations or warranties with respect to the accuracy or completeness of the contents of this work and specifically disclaim all warranties including, without limitation, warranties of fitness for a particular purpose. No warranty may be created or extended by sales or promotional materials. The advice and strategies contained in this book may not be suitable for every situation. This work is sold with the understanding that the publisher is not engaged in rendering legal, accounting, or other professional services. If professional assistance is required, the services of a professional person should be sought. Only ever accept Tax advice from a tax adviser, authorized by HMRC.

Neither the publisher nor the author shall be liable for damages arising here form. The fact that an organization or website is referred to in this work as a potential source of further information or support does not mean that the author or the publisher endorses the information the organization or website may provide or recommendations it may make. Further, readers should be aware that websites listed in this work may have changed or disappeared since this work was written, and that any specific fees or charges quoted may have changed.

© **2312 Books**
- April 1, 2020 -

Table of Contents

Introduction 7

Chapter 1: Foundations 9

The Business 9
    Core Functions 9
    Secondary Revenue Streams 10
    Growth 10

Equipment 11
    Projector 12
    Sound System/Speakers 13
    Projection Screen 13
        Roller Screens 13
        Fast Fold Projector Screens 13
        Inflatable 'Air' Screens 14
    Video Source 15
    Buying New vs Second Hand 15

Company Set-up 17
    Legal Status 17
    VAT Registration 17
    Bank Account 18
    Merchant Account 18
    Insurance 19
    Tax and Accounting 19

Chapter 2: Fundamentals 21

Film Classification 21
    The Classifications, and what they mean 21
    Recommendations 22
    Showing unclassified materials 22

Licenses 23
    Film Licenses 23

© 2312 Books
- April 1, 2020 -

Music Licenses 25
Premises License 25

Event Regulations 26

Chapter 3: Generating income 29

Selling Tickets 29
    Eventbrite 29
    Social Media 30
    Your Own Website 31
    Other Ticket Agencies 31
    Box Office / At the Venue 32
    Other options 32
    Cancellations and Refunds Policy 33

Marketing and Promotion 34
    Social Media 34
    Flyers and Posters 35
    Editorial and Local Media Advertising 36
    Mailouts 36
    Images and Copyright 36

Selling Advertising Space 37
    Opportunities 37
    Selling 37
    Preparing Artwork 38
    Creating Advertising Reels 39
    Video Adverts 39

Selling merchandise and other things 40

Chapter 4: Running Events 41

Planning 41
    Private Hire Events, Parties and Celebrations 41
        Information Gathering 41
        Film Selection 43
        Site Survey 43

  Bad Weather Contingency 44
  Written Agreement 44
 Ticketed Events 45
  Information Gathering 45
  Selecting the venue 46
  Constructing a deal with the venue 47
  Film Selection 48
  Site Survey 49
  Bad Weather Contingency 49
  Written Agreement 50
  Detailed Event Plan 50
  Promote the event 51
  Sell advertising space 51

Preparation 51
 Constructing the programme 51
  Film media 51
  Background music 52
  Compiling the advertising slideshow 52
  Trailers 52
  Video adverts and film shorts 53
 Putting it all together 53
 Rehearse, rehearse, rehearse 53
 Test everything 54

The Main Event 54
 Equipment Setup and Strike 54
 Private Hire 56
 Ticketed Events 57

Accounting 58

Profit and Loss of a Typical Event 59

Appendix: Useful Contacts 63

Index 67

Introduction

With the amazing summer weather we enjoyed in 2018, open air cinema has never been more popular, and is great entertainment for family and friends at private parties, corporate hospitality events, charity fundraiser, community cinema and open air festivals and events.

If you enjoy parties, meeting people and entertaining them, have you ever contemplated your own events business? Starting a Pop-Up Cinema is a great way to get into the entertainment industry at ground floor level, with a small initial investment in equipment, low risk and low overheads, there is great potential for a fun lifestyle business, with good income potential.

It is an ideal business to be run from home, without the overheads of a traditional static cinema building, a couple or sole trader can comfortably operate this business on a part time or full-time basis, with casual labour or, better still, friends and family, to provide additional help to erect the screen on event days.

It works well as seasonal business if you want to concentrate on open air events alone, or year-round if you do indoor events too. Careful selection of your equipment will allow for both indoor and outdoor use, so the choice is yours!

There are multiple income streams. As well as private hire fees, and ticket sales at your own events, supplementary income can be earned from selling popcorn, hot and cold food and drink, merchandise, advertising space to local businesses, and so on.

If you google 'pop up cinema hire' you will see the fees charged for hiring out equipment alone can be astronomical! It is common for customers to pay in excess of £1,000 for hiring the complete service (which includes the staff to build, operate and strike the equipment) for just one night! There is a huge profit margin running these events as the license and other costs are minimal.

You can charge anywhere from £10 to £25 for tickets to your own events and the gross profit can be as much as 60% of box office sales. For example, you set your ticket price at £10 and sell 100, your total box office is £1000, and up to £600 could be your gross profit, for ONE night's work!

Add to this any additional revenue derived from up selling other items, then multiply by the number of events you chose to host throughout the year, and you will see how profitable this can become with plenty of energy and enthusiasm to maximise ticket sales!

Apart from the actual operating of the equipment at performances there is inevitably some day-to-day paperwork to be done; licensing and returns; accounting; promotional activities; box office management, and so on.

This guidebook includes everything you need to know to set up and operate your new business, including the basics on legal structure and insurances, and detailed information on license requirements, ticket agency contacts, equipment recommendations, social media and traditional marketing. There are many excellent resources in the market place that will go into the details of setting up and running your own business, and this guide is an invaluable 'add on' to these with all the industry specific detail you need to get your own popup cinema up and running for the summer season!

Chapter 1: Foundations

This guide provides a complete description of your pop-up cinema business, its core processes and helpful advice on future growth potential, labour saving techniques and important business suppliers and contacts. It should be used as the basis for your own bespoke operations manual which will evolve over time, as you find better ways to do things, new opportunities to exploit and new suppliers and contacts.

Special attention must be paid to mandatory administration tasks, as these include licensing and reporting activities that are required by law and / or under the terms of various agreements with suppliers and governing bodies.

All information contained in this manual is accurate and true as of the date printed at the bottom of the Table of Contents. Legislation, licensing terms and, most specifically, license fees are subject to change.

The Business

Core Functions
As well as hosting ticketed open-air and indoor events in historic venues and gardens, the equipment and staff are available for hire to present cinema at private events, festivals, parties and charity fundraisers.

Primary revenue is derived from ticket sales at self-run events and private hire fees.

The ticket prices set depend on a number of factors including local demographics, the profile of the venue, and competition in the area, and are usually in the range £10 – £25 per ticket. Concessions are generally offered to minors, pensioners, early bird bookings etc.

Private hire fees depend on the nature of the event (i.e. private party, public non-ticketed events, charity fundraisers, etc.) and are usually in the range £500 - £1000 per day.

Secondary Revenue Streams

Additional revenue can be generated at self-run events, depending on the arrangements made with the host venue, in the sale of popcorn, hot and cold food and drink, merchandise, ponchos, chair and blanket hire, and in the selling of advertising space and sponsorship to local businesses. There are numerous third-party suppliers with whom to partner for these events.

Growth

The initial assets purchased when setting up the business should provide at least one complete set of equipment required to run open air and indoor cinema presentations. Once established, the purchase of a second set of equipment will allow for multiple events to be operated on the same nights, increasing income potential and providing backup in case of an equipment failure.

Larger screens and more advanced projectors will allow for larger audiences, extended hours of operation etc.

The 'dry hire' of **equipment only** for customers to operate themselves is common and easy money as there are no costs to the business other than delivery and collection. This should be avoided until a second complete set of equipment is available, and appropriate insurance in place to cover any loss or damage.

Equipment

The basic components required to operate the business at start-up comprises: -

- ✓ Projector
- ✓ Sound system/speakers
- ✓ Projection Screen
- ✓ Video source (probably an HD Blu-Ray player)
- ✓ Cables – all connection cables for above, plus a number of waterproof power extension reels (suggest 50m length)

Additional items desirable, but not essential to begin with: -

- ✓ A dedicated laptop (for running advertising reels, etc.)
- ✓ An MP3 or CD player (for background music)
- ✓ A web site and/or Social Media presence

To minimize your initial capital outlay you might consider hiring the equipment you need to start off with. This may be a valid choice if you are unsure of your chosen business and want to 'try it out' but it is not a sound long term strategy. You should be aware that daily hire costs are HUGE – commonly £1K or more, per hire for a complete setup. This is a good thing, of course, as you are starting a business where you, yourself, may be hiring out the equipment in future and reaping the rewards – but can be a massive drain on resources when putting on your first few presentations. You will need to do your sums very carefully to make sure that your projected ticket sales will cover the hire fees plus provide you with some benefit (either in profit, increased visibility or potential for follow up business to be generated).

You can expect to purchase a complete set of professional grade equipment for under **£10K**. As well as spreading the cost of that outlay over multiple events (for accounting purposes) you will have a set of depreciating assets that will retain some value should you decide to sell them on.

Resist the temptation to purchase cheap projectors, speakers and inflatable screens that may be listed for sale on auction sites, unless you are certain they are up to the job. Remember the proverb "if something appears too good to be true, it probably is". Equipment not designed for heavy duty professional use may not be robust enough to cope with the rigors of open-air cinema and may provide a poor viewing experience for your audience. If your audience has a bad experience, either through poor sound or picture quality, or cancellation due to equipment failure, you may lose their future custom.

Projector

A 5000 lumens (minimum) Full HD Projector, similar to the **NEC NP3250**, is recommended. **Lumens** are a measure of light visible to the human eye from the projector lamp. The higher the lumens, the brighter the projected image will be. In real world terms, anything with a value of 5000 lumens is suitable for use in reduced light environments (outdoors from approximately twilight) – although this also depends on the quality of the projection screen.

There are a mind-boggling array of features and options available, and you should do your research on the internet or seek professional advice as the correct projector for your needs – some helpful supplier contacts are listed in the Appendix.

Some key points to consider when selecting your device are;

- brightness (as discussed above)

- aspect ratio – standard 4:3, widescreen 16:9 (preferred), cinemascope 21:9

- maximum resolution (similar to TV terminology HD, 4K, 8K)

- keystone and lens shift capabilities - to 'correct' projected image shape distortion when projector is not able to be situated in the optimum position (i.e. centred at exactly 90 degrees in front, or behind the screen)

- 'Throw' – the distance that the projector can throw the image (i.e. the distance the projector must be placed away from the screen). Short throw projectors may seem a good choice for limiting the amount of space required for your set up, but they do not have the flexibility of longer throw projectors.

- Inputs – as a minimum you will require an input that matches your video source (for Blu-ray Players probably an HDMI and / or composite video connections). If you plan to use a laptop for playing advertising reels etc. you will need a compatible input on your projector and the ability to seamlessly switch between the laptop and Blu-ray player. Obviously, the wider array of inputs on your chosen projector, the greater flexibility it will afford you when trying out different video sources.

Sound System/Speakers

You will need at least two speakers, with integral or standalone amplification, and a basic mixer / processor unit, which will allow you to mix or switch between inputs from two or more audio sources. An example system is the **Alto Professional 1100 Wat 12" – 2way Powered, speakers, with integral amplifiers, and ZMX52 compact 5-channel Mixer.**

Consider a 3-speaker configuration, comprising centre, left and right speakers to provide comparable full cinema quality sound, or surround sound (4 plus speakers). You will need to be conscious though of carrying too much unnecessary equipment around with you. You will ideally start by transporting your entire pop up cinema around in your family estate car, and a 2-speaker setup is perfectly adequate, and will save valuable boot space. Again, there are many excellent resources on the internet where you can research the best sound system for your needs, and some helpful supplier contacts are listed in the Appendix.

Projection Screen

There are a variety of screen types available for the mobile cinema market, so it is worth spending a few moments describing the differences between them and why some will be more suitable than others.

Roller Screens

As the name suggests, these generally come complete, rolled in a tube which you pull up manually to extend the projection surface. Certainly, the most convenient to transport and setup (which can easily be done by one person alone), they are reasonably inexpensive to purchase and a good choice for indoor presentations to smaller audiences. The available screen sizes are limited, and the screen not suitable for outdoor presentations.

Fast Fold Projector Screens

These are basically rigid frames that come in kit form, with a detachable screen surface, which are assembled and disassembled for each presentation. Examples such as the **Projecta Fast Fold Deluxe** screens come in a variety of sizes up to approximately 8 metres wide and can accommodate larger audiences (<500). Ideally suited to indoor venues, they are safe for use outdoors also, with appropriate tethering (always follow manufacturers guidelines). They tend to look more professional, especially with optional drape (curtain) kits, but can be significantly more expensive than other screen types. They are more difficult and time consuming to setup, the larger screens requiring 3 or 4 people to put them up safely, and ship in large and heavy carry cases, so requiring a larger vehicle to transport them from site to site.

Inflatable 'Air' Screens

By far the most common choice for popup cinemas due to the comparative ease in which they can be transported and setup, the inflatable 'air' screens also come in a range of sizes from 3 to 16 metres wide, and can accommodate audiences up to 3000, or 250 cars (for drive-in cinema). The cheaper examples, such as the **Celexon Inflatable**, require a powered air pump to be fitted and running throughout the presentation to keep the frame inflated. Like a bouncy castle, a loss of power will result in the frame deflating before your very eyes. The noise of the air pump too is significant and precludes the use of these screens indoors, where the noise will likely reverberate around the room and distract from the overall experience for your audience.

Sealed-air versions, such as the **Airscreen Nano** range, are more expensive, but once inflated, are sealed and remain inflated without need of an air pump running in the background. As well as making this variation suitable for both indoor and outdoor use, it frees the screen from having to be positioned close to a power source, so allowing you to be more flexible with your site setups.

The cheaper inflatables may have permanently attached screen surfaces (to be avoided) or detachable, attached to the frame with Velcro. The more expensive will come with durable cable ties that attach to both frame and screen surface whilst deflated and pull tight into place as the frame is inflated.

Always select a frame with a detachable screen surface – this allows for easy cleaning and replacement should any damage occur.

Depending on the frame selected you may also have a choice as to the type of projection surface you buy; suitable for front projection; for projection from the rear or; for both. The surface is specially treated to provide the best possible picture quality from the direction you wish to project. If budget allows go for a surface that is optimized for both front and rear projection to provide you with maximum flexibility.

For best picture quality you should really project from the front on a front optimized screen. However, the positioning of the projector and associated hardware and cabling in front of the screen may block the view to part of your audience and will present safety issues that will need to be addressed. Projecting from the back presents a slightly degraded picture (unless you use a surface especially optimized for this alone) but keeps all equipment and cabling safely away from your audience.

All variations of inflatable screens must be properly tethered to the ground inside and out, following manufacturer guidelines, and only operated outdoors within prescribed wind speed limits.

NB. In order to be able to project from the rear your projector must offer this function. It must, in effect, be able to reverse the image being projected, so that from the front the image appears the correct way round.

Video Source

Initially a domestic Blu-ray player is more than adequate to play commercially available Blu-ray and DVD disks (subject to licensing, which is discussed later). You will require a standard HDMI connection into your chosen projector. Ideally, select a player that has analogue audio output connections too. This will allow you to connect the audio outputs direct to your sound mixer/speakers rather than have to go through the HDMI cable to the projector and out again.

A laptop may also be a video (and audio) source for advertising reels, pre-show trailers short films etc. and for background music. Depending on the laptop, connection to the projector may also be via HDMI, or via a number of other connectors. Connect the audio output (usually the external speaker or headphone socket on most laptops) direct to your sound mixer/speakers so you can seamlessly switch between audio sources. Check the manufacturer's documentation for details.

DCP Players, used in all Digital Cinemas, are becoming available in the portable market but are cost prohibitive when first starting out, unless you have very deep pockets indeed. These will project Digital Cinema Packages (DCP), electronic video files downloaded from the film distributer, and removes the need to wait for a film to be released to the domestic Blu-Ray market. This may give you a slight competitive edge, being able to play new movies ahead of other popup cinemas. However, DCP hardware can currently cost in the 'thousands of pounds' bracket, and not all newly released films are currently being made available to the portable market in this way, and certainly not while they are still showing in first-run cinemas, so the benefit is limited.

Buying New vs Second Hand

Good quality, reliable, well cared for second-hand equipment is no more or less likely to fail you than brand new and may be considerably cheaper to purchase up front. The benefit of new, of course, is the manufacturer's warranty that will be supplied with it, and which may save you money in the long run if repairs or replacements are required. However, you must read the small print very carefully and determine if anything you plan to do with the equipment may invalidate the warranty and result in hefty repair bills in any case. You will, for example, be transporting your equipment a lot, operating in cool, damp conditions (even on a balmy summer evening it gets cold and damp once the sun's gone down), even perhaps loaning it out to other people. If you end up having to fork out for repairs anyway then the additional outlay for the warranty may not have been worth it.

Consider too the terms of warranty repairs; will you have to return the unit for repair? how long will it take? will they provide a replacement etc.? It will not help you much if your projector fails a few days before your next scheduled presentation and you have to send it away for two weeks for repair and return.

In an ideal world you would purchase two of everything so if one device fails you on the day you can swap it out quickly and ensure that the show goes on, while the faulty unit gets repaired or replaced. However, initially, you will have to accept the risk that something beyond your control may go wrong that causes you to have to cancel a presentation at short notice. You can mitigate the risk by identifying local reliable repair shops where you can take your equipment for quick turn arounds and rental companies where you can hire replacement devices at short notice. As previously said, hiring equipment is very expensive and can negatively affect your income from an event if you have had to bring in emergency equipment but sometimes it is worth the financial hit to maintain your reputation and avoid sending home unhappy customers.

Company Set-up

Legal Status
Limited company or Sole Trader?

This is a low risk business model and apart from the initial investment doesn't require any major capital outlay. If you are sensible, the requirements and risks of credit and creditors are therefore minimal.

There are significant protections offered by forming and operating under a limited company, but the running costs are high. The accounting requirements demand qualified and expensive accountants and should be considered only if there are other factors that suggest incorporation might be the best option for your personal circumstances.

For a new business, operating as a sole trader or partnership on a self-employed basis is the most straight forward and cost-effective way to get started. Incorporation can always be done later if business income or expansion plans demand greater protection.

You should seek advice from HMRC and other professionals if you are uncertain as to the best option for you, and will need specialist assistance if you do wish to register a Limited Company.

VAT Registration
As of the time of writing, you must register for VAT if your VAT taxable turnover is, or is likely to be, more than £85,000 (the 'threshold') in a 12-month period. As a new business, unless you have other VAT taxable income from other self-employed business interests, you are unlikely to reach that threshold in the first couple of years of operation.

You can voluntarily elect to register for VAT if your income is below the threshold, for example if you plan to make large, regular purchases of goods and services, to be able to reclaim the VAT portion. This is unlikely unless or until you purchase significant stocks of merchandise or food stuffs to sell at events or significantly expand your equipment list.

Bear in mind that once VAT registered you MUST charge VAT on all hire fees and tickets that you sell. For normal ticket purchasers, who will not be VAT registered themselves, paying an extra 20% on the price of entry to your events may not go down too well…

It is best to delay VAT registration until you really *need* to do it. Check with HMRC for the most up-to-date advice.

Bank Account

You are well advised, even if operating as a self-employed sole trader, to have a dedicated bank account for all business related transactions. This will make book-keeping and tax returns much easier when the time comes.

Inevitably, at start-up, you will have to transfer some money into the account by way of a loan to cover initial expenditure. This can be easily identified and paid back when income allows, prior to any tax calculations.

As a new business, unless you have previously or currently run other business ventures, you may struggle to find high street banks that will provide business banking facilities to you. Cashplus, who are internet based, do provide basic banking to business and setting up an account can be done quickly and easily online with minimum fuss or credit checks. Although their service is limited (there are no chequebooks, branches etc.), you can receive and pay monies via their banking app 24 hours a day, transfer funds in and out and so on, the annual fee is low compared to high street banks. Check out their website for more details and to apply: www.cashplus.co.uk - Other providers of online business banking are available.

Merchant Account

Although you can sell tickets at events on a cash only basis, having credit card payment facilities will make life so much easier for your customers, and may encourage them to spend more on your merchandise and popcorn.

There are a number of providers of 'merchant accounts' and card readers, the best-known being PayPal. You can search 'card readers for small business' online and you will find comparisons out there.

iZettle provides a card reader, which tethers via Bluetooth to your smart phone or tablet, and an app to manage your credit card transactions. The initial one-off cost for the card reader is £29, and per transaction fees of 1.75% is among the lowest on the market. As with most of its competitors, there is no setup costs or lock-in contract, and money is deposited into your bank account within 1-2 days.

More details on iZettle can be found on their website www.iZettle.com

Insurance

You are well advised to have adequate insurance to cover the loss or damage of equipment used for the business. This is especially true if you 'dry hire' the equipment and do not supervise the use of it at all times.

Your standard home contents and motor insurance policies may not cover the storage and transportation of equipment for business purposes so you should consider increasing cover accordingly.

At the very least, you should take out public liability insurance. An inflatable screen will be large and could cause injury if not tethered down correctly or operated outside of prescribed wind speed limits. Venues, especially council runs facilities, may well insist you provide evidence of public liability insurance. Liability up to £4m is usually sufficient.

You may need to shop around to get the best quotes for business insurance. Pop-Up Cinema businesses do not often crop up on the drop-down lists of online insurance brokers and are treated with some caution by insurers as the business is still very new and not known to them.

Some helpful supplier contacts are listed in the Appendix.

Tax and Accounting

It goes without saying that you must always keep a full record of income and expenditure as it will make filing tax returns much easier! If you have access to a bookkeeper, then so much the better, however software applications like QuickBooks, make invoicing and record keeping for the novice as straight forward as possible.

If you are operating under a Limited Company, you will need to submit annual returns and must get your accounts certified by an accountant. Please refer to the HMRC website for further information on requirements for Limited Companies.

For self-employed Sole Traders and Partnerships, you will need to complete annual Self-Assessment tax returns. In the first instance you will need to inform HMRC that you are now self-employed, provide basic information on the name and nature of your business and your start date. You will be advised on how to register for online self-assessment. If you are receiving other taxable income or benefits beyond income generated by this business, you may need to seek help completing your first tax return.

You should always refer to an authorized Tax Adviser or HMRC on all matters relating to tax.

Chapter 2: Fundamentals

With the business infrastructure in place, you can now concentrate on the details of running your pop-up cinema business. Like traditional cinema and events-based businesses, you will be subject to various licensing laws, regulations and restrictions, so you should understand these before hosting your first event. The headlines are discussed in this chapter, but please research these in more detail on the internet and regularly update yourself as regulations change and you will need to stay on top of them.

Film Classification

All feature films, short films and trailers which are shown theatrically in the UK must be classified by the British Board of Film Classification (BBFC), unless permission has been granted by the local authority in the area that the work is being shown. You must be aware of what each classification means as the law applies equally to open air cinemas for both your own ticketed events and private hire bookings.

The Classifications, and what they mean

U	U Universal – Suitable for all Suitable for audiences aged 4 and over
PG	PG Parental Guidance. General viewing allowed but some scenes may be unsuitable for young children.
12a	12A – Suitable for 12 years and over. No child under the age of 12 may view the film in a cinema unless accompanied by an adult.
12	12 – Suitable for 12 years and over. Specific rating for the sale and rental of DVDs and Blurays. No child under the age of 12 may buy or rent a 12 rated film.
15	15 – Suitable only for 15 years and over. No one younger than 15 may see a 15 film in the cinema.

18	18 – Suitable only for adults. No one younger than 18 may see an 18 film in the cinema.
R18	R18 – to be shown in specially licensed cinemas only. R18 films contain explicit materials for adults only and may not be publicly presented anywhere outside of specially licensed premises or private home.

Recommendations

Always make sure that you know the film classification of the film you plan to present. This will usually be quoted on the film license booking confirmation, but you can search the BBFC website (www.bbfc.co.uk) for your chosen film if in any doubt. Also check the classification on the actual DVD or Blu-ray as this can sometimes differ (if the film has been re-edited or re-classified since initial release). Where they differ <u>always</u> assume the most restrictive rating and plan accordingly.

You must clearly state the film classification on all posters, flyers, website and ticket sales listings, and at the venue. Also, brief anyone tasked with selling tickets face to face at the venue or other outlets so they know to inform customers of any age restrictions prior to purchasing tickets. This is especially important for 15 rated films and over.

On the night, make sure everyone is aware of any age restriction and is ready to deal with any problems. 'Mystery shoppers' have been known to attend open air events to check out procedures to observe the age ratings.

Whenever possible, stick to films rated 12a and below. They are far better suited to open air 'family' events, and a lot less hassle to control. Occasionally, a 15 rated film may be really big news in the cinema, and you will want to show it, so just be aware of the additional overhead required.

For private hire bookings, your customer may have requested a specific film, rated 15 or above. You should advise your customer that all guests must meet the minimum age requirements and put the necessary checks in place.

Showing unclassified materials

As already stated, all films, short films and trailers shown theatrically (in cinemas, including open air cinemas) must be classified and you should take care to select only classified materials when sourcing film trailers and short films to add to your programme.

However, for private hire bookings you may present materials supplied by the customer (trade films, wedding videos etc.) at private parties, conferences and celebrations, and as long as the audience have not had to purchase tickets to attend.

For all public events where tickets are sold, including charity fundraisers, any materials should be submitted to the BBFC for classification or permission granted by the local authority.

Licenses

Each time you screen a film, you will need to buy a license that gives you the right to screen it. For public performances you will also need to have a music license if you plan to play recorded music before or after the presentation and the venue itself does not already have one. In addition, the venue must be licensed for public entertainment. If it is not you will need a Temporary Events Notice.

To better explain this, consider a traditional cinema; it is required to hold a (commonly referred to as) public entertainment license, paid to the council, allowing it to open its doors to the public in order to entertain them. It also requires a music license, paid to the music licensing body, to allow it to play recorded 'background' music in its bars, public areas and in the auditorium before and after the film presentation. Finally, it also needs a film license, paid to the film distributor, in order to publicly present that distributors film on a specified date(s).

As a popup cinema you are required to hold the same licenses. Often the venue at which you are presenting will already hold 'public entertainment' and music licenses, meaning you only need to worry about the film licenses. Sometime though they will not, and you will have to apply for temporary licenses to cover your activities.

Film Licenses

Every time you screen a film, you will need to buy a license that gives you the right to screen it. The exact cost of the license depends on a few factors including whether you, or the customer hiring you, are selling tickets to your screening. The good news is, obtaining the license is, in most cases, very straightforward.

There are a number of distributors, including the BFI, Filmbank and MPLC, through which you can obtain a single title screening license (STSL) for most films that commercially available on DVD or Blu-ray.

Filmbank provides a very quick and easy application process and has a huge catalogue of movies available to license online, including nearly all the most recent releases. Please go to their website www.filmbankmedia.com to review their terms and conditions and to register with them. You will need to pay an initial deposit, currently £150, which is refundable if or when you close your account with them.

For indoor presentations, you simply create a new booking online, select your choice of film and provide details of the date, venue, ticket prices (etc.). You will normally receive confirmation that your booking has been approved within 2-3 days. The fee will also be confirmed at this point but does not become payable until after the performance date.

For open air presentations, you currently must download a form, complete it manually, then email it back to Filmbank. Confirmation of approval can take up to 2 weeks. Again, the license fee will be confirmed at this point, and the booking added to your online account.

You can cancel bookings at any point up to the day of the performance without any financial penalty.

After the event you will need to log back in to your Filmbank account and, for ticketed performances, complete a 'return' which confirms the total box office receipts. An invoice is then raised and payable within 7 days.

License costs are subject to change but, at time of writing, start at £139 or 35% of total box office receipts (whichever is the greater) plus VAT, per presentation.

You can purchase the DVD or Blu-ray of the film from Filmbank but are likely to be able to source them cheaper from Amazon or eBay yourself. DCP format copies of special release titles (i.e. those not yet released on DVD or Blu-ray) are available to download for some titles, but additional hardware is required to be able to play these.

In some circumstances your private hire customer may request a film that is not in the Filmbank library and so is not as easy to license. Check the BFI and MPLC catalogues to determine if the titles are available through them. If not, you can use FindAnyFilm.com to search for who owns the rights to the film you want to show, then search online for relevant contact details – you will need to provide them with as much information as you can about your proposed presentation. Fees and response times from individual distributors will vary greatly.

You must not begin promoting or selling tickets for any film presentation until license approval has been confirmed.

Music Licenses

Previously two different licenses covered the use of live and recorded music: PRS (Performing Right Society) and PPL (Phonographic Performance Limited). Thankfully the two merged in 2018 creating 'TheMusicLicense' making registration and compliance much simpler.

If the venue you are using holds other public events; weddings, concerts, theatre performances and so on, it is likely that they already have a blanket music license that covers them throughout the year. If they do not, you will need to have a license yourself to cover your own music usage on that day.

There are a range of tariffs for 'TheMusicLicense', and the one relevant to popup cinemas is the 'General Purpose' tariff. Please refer to the PPL PRS website www.pplprs.co.uk for full details and to apply for an account to be setup. You will need to pay a small fee for each screening (around £7 per 100 audience members), and you will be asked to estimate and pay this in advance for the year ahead or in instalments.

Always check with the venue first to see if they have relevant music licenses in place.

Premises License

Not to be confused with the Film License, which permits you to present a specific film title in public on a given date, a premises (or public entertainments) license is required at each venue to allow for any public performance at that venue. You are not permitted to hold a public performance of any kind unless the venue is licensed appropriately.

Generally speaking, you will select venues (stately homes, church halls, community theatres, wedding venues) that hold public events throughout the year, so they will, most likely, already hold a premises license that allows you to present a film there. Occasionally however, you may choose, or be asked, to present in an unusual or unique location (a beach, museum, castle ruin, etc.) that is not itself licensed for public performance. This is not necessarily a problem.

In these instances, you or the venue may submit to the local authority a Temporary Events Notice (TEN) if your venue is in England or Wales; or an Occasional License if your venue is in Northern Ireland or Scotland. This allows you to gain permission for various licensable activities (including public performance, sale of food, drink and merchandise etc.) at a specific location for one event (single or multiple consecutive dates).

Costs and where to apply

For locations in England and Wales, the current fee, at time of writing, per Temporary Event Notice is £21. See https://www.gov.uk/temporary-events-notice for full details.

Scotland, the current fee per Occasional License is £10. https://www.gov.uk/occasional-licence-scotland

Fees in Northern Ireland are variable depending on the size of the audience. https://www.gov.uk/occasional-licence-northern-ireland

Note: You can apply to sell alcohol at your event via the same Temporary Event Notice, but you will also need to hold a **personal alcohol license** if you intend to do this yourself, and the council may impose additional conditions upon their approval.

Event Regulations

Like all businesses, you are required to observe certain rules and regulations surrounding health and safety and other matters when holding public events. You should be aware of the law, and how it will affect you:

- Health and Safety at Work etc. Act 1974 (HASWA)
    - specifically, you must ensure that no employees, or members of the public are exposed to risks to their health and safety at your events
    - this requires you perform a risk assessment at the venue prior to your event taking place
- there are specific requirements that all venues must meet, including, but not limited to;
    - sufficient space for the public to move safely around
    - routes and exits must be unobstructed
    - car parks, footpaths and all staging/structures must be suitable for use in wet weather
    - there must be adequate emergency lighting
    - access for people with disabilities and limited mobility
    - adequate fire safety checks

- up to date electrical installations and lighting checks
- available drinking water
- sufficient toilets: -
  1 toilet per 100 females
  1 toilet per 500 males + 1 urinal per 150 males
- hand washing facilities
- rubbish and recycling bins

- first aid management
  - a qualified first aider should be in attendance at all small events
  - ideally every event should have at least 2 first aiders.
    The voluntary first aid society may provide a First Aid Post staffed by qualified first aiders

- stewards, security and CRB checks
  - there must be an appropriate number of stewards and supervisors for the security and control of the site and the attending public.
  - consider whether stewards need to be licensed by the Security Industry Authority - this will depend on audience numbers, whether alcohol is a significant part of the event, and may be a requirement of the local authority when granting you a Temporary Event Notice (TEN).
  - the Criminal Records Bureau (CRB), vets applications for people who want to work with children and vulnerable adults. If your audience will include unaccompanied children or vulnerable adults, you should verify that all staff are CRB checked.

- noise control

  You need to consider not only the noise that you will make with background music and film soundtrack, but also any noise disturbance caused by your audience, setting up and striking the set, and so on. Many locations will have strict noise level limits or hours of operations (i.e. all music to be ended by 11pm).

- food safety

  If you will be selling food yourself at your events you will need to be aware of and comply with the Food Safety Act 1990.

- maximum wind speed for open air operation of your cinema screen

  The erection of temporary structures at entertainment events falls within the definition of "construction work" in Regulation 2(1) of the Construction

(Design and Management) Regulations 2007 (CDM). Your equipment should be designed to withstand gusts of wind up to 24mph, but please check the manufacturers documentation supplied with your screen for updated guidance. It is not safe to operate with windspeeds above the maximum recommended by the manufacturer. Doing so may invalidate your warranty and public liability insurance, and could present a real danger to your staff and audience.

For more information, you should read;

The Event Safety Guide: A guide to health, safety and welfare at music and similar events. HSG195 (1999) HSE Books ISBN 9 780 717 624 539.

Chapter 3:
Generating income

So, now your business is setup, you understand the basics of film classifications, licensing and the legal requirements of running events, you need to start earning some money. The two main opportunities for generating income are by hiring yourself and your equipment out for private events and hosting your own ticketed film presentations. Prior to organising your first event, you will need to understand the ways in which you can promote yourself and sell tickets and other merchandise.

Selling Tickets

When hosting your own film presentations your primary source of income will be through the sale of tickets. Unlike traditional fixed location cinemas, you probably won't have the luxury of a permanently manned box office, so will need to sell tickets in a variety of other ways to maximize earning potential.

Eventbrite

Your primary internet-based ticket agency should be Eventbrite, although other online ticket resellers are available and are discussed later.

There are no upfront fees for using Eventbrite. However, there is a per ticket sold charge applied. This charge can either be paid by you or passed on to the ticket buyer.

Up to date list of fees are available on their website, but are currently £0.49 + 4% per ticket (ex. VAT).

To register go to their website www.eventbrite.co.uk, click **Create Event,** then **Get Started** to create your company profile. You will need to provide details of the bank account you wish to use to receive income from your events.

Online help will assist you to create your first event. You will need to setup a record for the venue/location first, then you can create an event and link to the venue page. When creating your venue and event remember to provide as much information as possible about the event itself including ticket price(s), times, age restrictions, facilities, parking arrangements etc. and keep a copy of everything. You will be inputting this information into your own website, and other ticket agency sites too!!

The money for all tickets sold is held by Eventbrite until after the event has taken place and there is a simple cancellation and refund process in place to return money to the customer if issues arise. Eventbrite will remit all monies due, minus any per ticket charges, within 7 days after the performance.

Review the standard terms and conditions of purchase they offer the ticket buyer and customize to your own needs if necessary. Their standard terms should be more than adequate for most scenarios. Configure the start and end dates for ticket sales. Notification for all sales will come to you by email and a full list of attendees made available when tickets sales end for that event. It is wise to close internet sales shortly before the event itself so that you have time to download / print the attendee list ready to check off on the door. Make sure within your listing that you explain tickets will still be available to purchase on the door once internet sales have closed, unless of course you are sold out, when you should update the listing accordingly.

Social Media

Facebook, Twitter and Instagram are very valuable marketing and sales tools. You should have your own business pages on each of these platforms and make regular posts to attract and inform your customer base.

When you create your event in Eventbrite, you are given the opportunity to post these direct to Facebook and Twitter and need to supply your login names/password and business page details for each. Once posted your social media followers will automatically be able to see your upcoming events and will be presented with a **Buy Tickets** button direct from the social media posts. This is an incredibly effective and cheap way to market and sell tickets if you already have lots of followers.

To build followers and to post your events on Social Media to a wider audience you can choose to 'boost your post' and select your target audience by location, demographic, interests etc. You set your budget and duration for a single post boost and Facebook/Twitter will continue to push your post to your target audience until the budget is spent. As a guide a budget of around £20 spread over a 4-week period should get your event seen by 5 – 10,000 people (depending on selection criteria used). If just 1% of those go on to buy tickets from that post, you could sell up to 100 tickets without any other advertising.

In the early days you will spend money boosting posts to reach your audience. The trick is to get them to like or follow your social media pages. Then, you can communicate with them over and over again at no cost. Once you have established a few thousand followers on your social media pages you should never have to boost posts again.

Your Own Website

If you have your own website, you will need to post event details there too. You may link listings direct to your Eventbrite event for purchasing tickets or have your own bespoke ticketing system.

Warning: If you have your own bespoke ticketing solution and receive payments directly from your customers you will need to have considered your cancellation and refund policies very carefully. You will need to ensure that all money is available to be refunded should the worst happen, and that any payment processing fees (credit card or PayPal fees for example) are also returned.

Other Ticket Agencies

There are many ticket agencies that you can use to post your events to. Each have their own fee structures and benefits.

www.designmynight.com – are an excellent London based ticketing site, who run regular marketing campaigns to their 1000s of subscribers. Less successful for events out in the regions, they are worth using for events anywhere in the Greater London and commuter belt region.

www.wegottickets.com – again have good marketing capabilities, best for live events and concerts but list pop up cinema events too.

www.skiddle.com – again, best for live events and concerts but the more unusual 'event' pop-up cinema nights go down well on here.

www.groupon.co.uk – great to list time limited discounts (i.e. flash sales 20% off etc.) if ticket sales are otherwise a bit sluggish. They are a terrible company for getting in contact with and setting up the deals in the first place. But once established, promotions work really well.

There is nothing to stop you listing your events on any or all of these sites at the same time. Just keep an eye on the number of tickets sold across all channels. Once you are nearing your maximum capacity for the event you should close the additional channels down so that you do not over sell.

Be consistent across all ticket agency sites. Make sure all event details, prices, terms and conditions are the same across all websites.

Box Office / At the Venue

You will of course want to be able to sell tickets to 'walk-ins' – those people who turn up without pre-booked tickets. You should have a desk and chair set up at the entrance and a supply of numbered paper tickets to sell on the door.

There are many online printing companies that can supply branded tickets, www.saxoprint.co.uk for example has a selection of templates you can use 'out of the box' or you can purchase generic tickets from everyday office suppliers. The important thing is you must be able to track how many tickets are sold for accounting purposes.

If your venue is open to the public and has its own shop or ticket office facilities, you could negotiate them selling tickets in advance on your behalf. There may or may not be a fee for doing this (i.e. a percentage of the ticket price) so you will need to weigh up the cost against the increased sales potential to see if it is worth it. From experience, it is always beneficial to have some face to face ticket sales available if possible. Open air cinema is largely an impulse buy, if the sun is shining when the customer reads your flyer or poster, they will buy tickets there and then if they are available. If they go home and have to go online to buy tickets, they may have already had time to change their minds!

Other options

You should consider extending your face-to-face selling opportunities as much as you can. Approach local tourist information centres, pubs and newsagents and see if they will sell tickets for you. Again, you may need to offer incentives for doing this (i.e. a percentage of the ticket price, free or discount tickets for themselves, free advertising for their business, etc.)

You will need to keep track of the number of paper tickets provided to each outlet so that when you return to reclaim the unsold tickets and get the money you can ensure everything is correct. You should also be able to identify from where each ticket has come, so customize them in some way for each outlet you use. This will help you identify the most fruitful places to place tickets the next time, and to work out the value of any benefits promised to the outlet for selling them.

Cancellations and Refunds Policy

Eventbrite and other ticket agency sites will supply you with generic terms and conditions of sale for tickets purchased from their sites. These will probably be sufficient for your needs. However you should consider your cancellations and refunds policies carefully, and ensure they are consistently communicated and applied across all sales channels.

Refunds

You may think that a no refunds policy is perfectly acceptable on all tickets purchased as this is standard practice in the theatre and large chain cinemas and can be justified if you consider that in the case of a poorly selling event (and there will always be some) the refund of a handful of tickets may make the difference between a small profit or no profit at all. However, this can seem unfair to the customer who may have a genuine reason why they can no longer attend your event and might dissuade them from attending your events in the future. It is sensible to offer refunds in certain circumstances.

For online ticket sales you should consider setting a time limit of no less than 7 days prior to performance up to which point the customer can request and receive a refund. This threshold is set on a per event basis and can be any number you want.

The threshold you set may depend on your arrangement with the venue in part. If your agreement is such that ticket sales must reach a certain level by a certain date to ensure that the event goes ahead then you will want to make sure that no-one can request a refund after that date.

If you offer refunds on online ticket sales, you will need to do the same for paper tickets purchased in advance. You will have to agree the refunds process with any outlets you use to sell tickets face to face. Some venues will have their own refunds policy and you will need to accommodate that. For example, they may offer refunds on any tickets they sell *only* if they can resell them.

Cancellations

You must make your cancellation policy clear and consistent on all sales channels. In general, should you need to cancel the event for any reason, you would refund all tickets purchased and associated fees without question, but you may consider offering to exchange tickets for another presentation if you can arrange another date at the same or nearby venue within a reasonable timeframe.

You must make clear what your policy is regarding the weather. You would normally not cancel a presentation unless to continue would be unsafe for you or the audience, the key indicator being wind speed. Generally, 24mph is the maximum speed at which you should operate your inflatable cinema screen but refer to the handbook provided with your screen for current guidelines. Above that, and you should cancel the performance on safety grounds.

You can operate safely in light rain conditions, and you could take the opportunity to upsell ponchos, and rent blankets if its colder than expected. You should take care to cover any electrical equipment to protect them from excess water. You don't want to cancel and give money back unless you really must, and with the vagaries of the British weather, it is inevitable you are going to be rained on sometimes! However, if the forecast is heavy rain and likely to be unpleasant for everyone you are better off postponing the event and trying again. A bad experience for your audience will mean they never come out again, and you want them to come back to you time and time again!

Marketing and Promotion

By using online ticket agency websites and Facebook events you are already promoting your film presentations to a wide audience of internet enabled and social media savvy customers. However, there is more you can do to reach out to other, less computer literate, customers, and to promote the private hire element of your business.

Social Media

As already discussed, you can promote your ticketed events and services to your social media followers, and boost posts to reach a wider audience, tailored to specific areas, gender, age group or interest.

Anyone following your social media pages will see anything you post at no cost to you. But when you are starting out you will have few if any followers so you will need to boost posts to get the word out. The trick is to build up your list of followers as quickly as possible so that you do not have to continue to pay for social media advertising for very long.

As well as boosting your first few events you should consider boosting other posts about your business, services and informational articles on popup cinema and movies in general. In each post provide a reason why the reader should start following your page(s). Offer incentives perhaps, competitions, regular film news updates etc. – anything to convince them to 'sign up'. When they do, that is one less person you must pay to advertise to next time round.

Do not neglect the Private Hire element of your business – it is after all the easiest way to make a profit without any of the hassle of selling tickets and promoting your event. Regular posts on this to as wide an audience as possible will help sow the seed and persuade people to hire you for their parties and special events.

Flyers and Posters

There is still no substitute for having well-designed and eye-catching flyers and posters stuck up at various locations around the venue and local shopping areas. They will drum up plenty of interest and are the most effective way of selling tickets to the spontaneous buyer, especially if there is somewhere onsite, they can purchase tickets there and then.

Flyers can be distributed door to door (but this is very time consuming and costly if you outsource it) or placed in piles at suitable local outlets where lots of people meet (coffee shops, pubs, clubs, train stations, libraries, colleges, universities etc.) Posters should be placed in local shop windows, tourist information centres and at the venue itself.

In the days prior to the event, street promotion is always a good way to sell last minute tickets. Always wear a high viz jacket with your logo clearly displayed and target high foot fall areas near the venue like busy markets, train and bus stations, and so on. Hand out flyers and have a supply of tickets available to sell to the spontaneous buyer.

Desktop applications such as Serif Page Plus are very simple to use and you can design and prepare your own artwork for A5 Flyers, and various posters sizes (A3 or A4 being the easiest to place in shop windows and on notice boards.)

If you open an account with an online print company, such as Saxoprint (www.saxoprint.co.uk) you can place an order for the amount of flyers or posters you want, upload the print ready PDF file and they will deliver the flyers direct to your door, usually within 3 to 5 days. They provide templates and print specification details on their website. Alternatively, search for a print company that also provides a design service and have the artwork created for you.

Editorial and Local Media Advertising

You should attempt to get free editorial coverage in the local news media. Research the local newspapers, radio stations and whats on guides and send out press releases for each film presentation.

You may need to pay for an advertisement in the local newspaper or free magazine to establish a relationship with them. They will then be more likely to support your future efforts with free editorial.

Mailouts

Your website should have a 'Subscribe to Newsletter' function to collect email addresses from people willing to receiving email marketing from you. You should also encourage people who purchase tickets from you on the door and via other means to subscribe to your website so they can be the first to hear about any new film presentations in their area.

You can email your subscribers every time you publish a new event direct from your website. There are still people out there who avoid Social Media, but who are happy to receive communications by email!

There are regulations surrounding the sending of marketing emails which you must observe. As a minimum you must allow your subscribers to opt out of receiving emails at any time.

Images and Copyright

You must not begin marketing your film presentation or selling tickets until you have received confirmation that the license has been approved. Filmbank provide a useful facility where you can download original poster artwork for most films in its catalogue. Where they are not available you can search the internet to find suitable images to use in your advertising and poster artwork. But take care to only use the original posters or publicity stills published by the film company to promote that film. The rights to all images generally belong to the person who created them and where film companies are happy for you to use their artwork to sell tickets to their films, other rights holders may not be. If in doubt as to where the image originated, check the copyright notice against the image you wish to use to see what is and isn't allowed.

You should not materially change any poster artwork you download but can incorporate it within your own design.

Selling Advertising Space

Cinema advertising is said to have 8 times greater impact than television, and can be much more localised, bringing enormous benefit to businesses in the immediate vicinity of the film presentation. Where private hire fees and ticket sales are the key income streams for your business, a secondary, very lucrative stream exists in the sale of advertising space and sponsorship to local and national businesses.

Opportunities

Pre-show advertising provides a fantastic opportunity to businesses to get their message across to a uniquely captive and attentive audience. No channel hopping, no getting up to make the tea – just a room (or lawn) full of cinemagoers intently watching the screen waiting for the trailers and main feature to begin!

You will generally have a window of perhaps 30 minutes prior to the start of the film in which you can run a slideshow of static advertisements. Each advert can remain on screen for between 20 seconds and 1 minute at a time and can loop round multiple times.

To work out how many advertising slots you have available to sell for each performance use the following formula;

Time Available ÷ (Advert Duration x Number of Loops)

Example: You have 30 minutes (1,800 seconds) available to run adverts, each advert will stay on screen for 30 seconds at a time, and you want it to loop round 3 times. The calculation would be 1800 ÷ (30 x 3) = 20. So, you can sell a maximum of 20 advertising slots for each performance.

Based on the above calculation, if you were able to sell 20 slots at £75 each, you would make an additional £1,500 for one performance alone over and above ticket sales.

You can also sell sponsorship deals: You can run static or video advertisements for one company, include their branding on your posters and merchandise, deck your screen and box office desk in their flags and banners, and so on.

Selling

The opportunities for selling advertising space are limited only by your imagination, but it is not that easy! You will need to have an aptitude for selling in order to generate good income.

Consider how attractive the proposition will be to local businesses when planning your events; historic or prestigious locations will attract more interest; the film itself may attract some advertisers more than others; estimated audience numbers and demographic are also key.

Small independent businesses are always looking for new ways to advertise and are usually more than happy to pay a reasonable amount for advertising. You will need to explain that this is a great way to bring in new customers and extend their reach to the local community.

Estate agents, solicitors, accountants, beauty salons, restaurants all usually set aside a budget for local advertising.

You will build up a database of local advertisers over time, and it is best to start emailing out and calling at least 2 weeks before a screening, and then again 2/3 days before to fill any last-minute slots.

You can set your advertising rates at a level you think you will be able to sell. As a start-up the following figures are achievable:

£75 for a single slide

£40 for a half page

£150 for a double (two page) advert

You can offer discounts on your standard fees for multiple adverts. It will be easier to sell adverts for a season of films as the combined audience numbers will be much higher.

You would not normally sell advertising space for private hire engagements.

You must consider your terms and conditions carefully. You should always require full payment in advance, as once the advert has been shown you would not want to have to chase for late payments. No payment = no advert. Also, if the presentation is cancelled, rather than postponed or rescheduled, will you refund the advertisers or roll their advert on to the next available presentation?

Preparing Artwork
As is usual with print media publications, when selling advertising space, you could require the advertiser to supply their own artwork. You would provide them with the technical specification and a deadline by which the artwork needs to be with you.

Finished artwork should be at least 1600px wide by 900px with a resolution of 300dpi minimum, prepared as image files in JPG, PNG, TIFF, EPS or PDF formats.

If you have graphic design skills, you could offer to design advertisements for the clients too. You may or may not be able to charge extra for this, but it would certainly help make a sale to a customer not able to create their own artwork.

There are plenty of graphic design companies and freelancers out there who will create artwork for you, but you would need to factor their rate into the cost you charge your customer.

Creating Advertising Reels

Once you have your complete set of artwork images you can insert them into your PowerPoint slideshow.

Create a template that includes basic slides into which you can insert your artwork and has simple slide transition animation and delay set for standard usage. You can re-use this over and over again.

Once completed, you can run the slideshow directly from within PowerPoint on the night or save the slideshow as a video (MPG) file and run that standalone.

Video Adverts

You can also have the capabilities to run video adverts, film shorts etc. and will no doubt be approached by film students, creatives and charities to present their films as part of your programme.

You will be able to play MPG and MP4 videos from your laptop, and can use Window Media Player software to put together a playlist of video files to run automatically one after the other. You would play your slideshow first, followed by any supplied video adverts, then trailers and so on.

You will need to make sure the content of all videos supplied is age appropriate. If you are playing the latest Disney movie for example, with a rating of U or PG, your adverts should be suitable for that audience only.

Selling merchandise and other things

At your events you may want to offer anything from Popcorn, soft drinks and snacks to hot food and alcohol, where this is permitted by the venue and relevant license. You may want to consider outsourcing some of this to third parties to begin with.

The sale of hot food and alcohol have additional licenses and legislation to worry about, and unless you are already experienced in those areas, you will not want to get bogged down in all that. The good news is there are plenty of event catering businesses around who will do all that for you. You can earn income either by way of a split of their proceeds, or a straight fee from the third party for attending your event.

Popcorn, which always adds the authentic cinema feel, can be purchased in pre-packed bags of cooked popcorn, or you could hire a popcorn machine and cook it onsite.

Merchandise such as flashing lights and torches, masks, fidget spinners etc. are readily available to purchase in bulk online and can be resold for a massive mark up.

There is a handy list of some suppliers to get you going in the Appendix.

Chapter 4: Running Events

Having now learned all the background information needed to put on your first event, we come to the key processes; event planning, operation and accounting.

Planning

The planning required depends on the type of event and whether it is your own ticketed event or a private hire booking.

Private Hire Events, Parties and Celebrations

Private hire events tend to be quite straightforward; often you are supplying one element of a larger event and much of the leg work is done by the customer and/or their own event planner. However, you will be responsible for delivering your part of the event and ensuring what you do is safe and legal. When tickets are to be sold for the event, even if by the customer (for a charity fundraiser as an example) rather than yourself, you will need to follow the **Ticketed Events** process.

Information Gathering

On receipt of the initial enquiry, you will need to obtain as much information as possible from the customer in order to provide a firm quotation. This should include;

- Nature of event
  (i.e. film night, birthday party, wedding, charity fundraisers etc.)
- Date, or selection of dates, and time.
- Venue Details
- Expected number of guests
- Age of any guests 15 or under
- Film preference (if any)
- Event Planner contact (if applicable)

- Main point of contact

You will need to determine what licenses you need to include in the quotation.

- Are tickets to be sold?
  If so, your quotation should include the minimum license fee payable, with a clause stating that a further charge will be payable at the end of the event, calculated against total box of returns.

- Does the venue have Premises and Music Licenses, are they applicable, or are they being arranged by the customer/customer event planner?
  - events in private homes where attendance is free do not require either.
  - you may not be required to play background music before the presentation, and therefore licensing for music not your concern.

You'll also need to identify any other costs you will need to factor in:

- How many staff do you need to do the job?
  Generally you will not need 'front of house' people to sell tickets at private events unless asked to supply them. But you still need a minimum of 2 people to setup and strike the equipment at the end of the event. If the customer wants you to supply additional people for meet-and-greet and other roles you will need to add those costs in.

- Do they want you to supply 'extras', like popcorn, refreshments, themed merchandise etc.?
  You may need staff to sell these for you, or provide them to each guest as part of the overall fee (i.e. one box of popcorn 'free' for each guest),

- Do you require to hire or purchase any additional equipment to do the job?
  Generators (if there is no suitable power source at the location), earphones and transmitter (for 'silent' cinema), different sized projector screen for larger or smaller audience numbers, chairs, blankets and so on.

The quotation you provide should always be subject to site survey (discussed below).

Film Selection

Your customer will often have a specific film in mind when they contact you to make a booking. You will need to explain that you cannot guarantee their choice until you have applied for and received confirmation of the license to show it.

Film studios will often place a temporary embargo on some of their titles which means you may not necessarily be able to obtain a license for a specific film, even if you have done so successfully before.

Be ready to suggest alternative titles appropriate for their event. When doing so consider film classifications and avoid 15 rated films and above unless you are certain that there will be no underage attendance.

Do your homework first – there is no point suggesting a film title that you cannot get a license for. You will become familiar with the Filmbank film catalogue and have a few titles that you show regularly and know are crowd pleasers. Before suggesting anything else, check the catalogue to make sure they are currently available.

If the client has a very specific requirement and the film is not listed on the Filmbank catalogue you can, as previously discussed, apply for a license directly to the distributer. However, response times and success in obtaining a license cannot be guaranteed and may put the event at risk if the event date is near.

Once you have agreed a film choice with the customer put the license application in immediately. It does not cost anything to apply, and you may cancel the booking without penalty at any point up to the scheduled date should the event change or not go ahead at all. Once the license is approved you can confirm the film with your customer.

Site Survey

In order to safely and comfortably set up and operate your equipment on site you will need to have;

- two dedicated power sockets no more than 50m (or maximum length of your power extension cables) from the location
- enough space to erect the screen with at least 10m air gap behind (if back projecting) and in front, in addition to being able to accommodate the audience comfortably.
- easy access to the site to set-up and strike the equipment
- facilities such as car parking and toilet

You will also need to look at the location and consider how best to layout the equipment and seating areas to provide the best possible experience for the audience.

Refer to the Event Regulations section in Chapter 2 of this guide for more details on what to consider.

Perform a risk assessment. Basically, walk around the site looking for potential issues. For example, the location of the power sockets in relation to where the screen and projector are set up might require cables to be laid across public walkways, your equipment might block an official fire escape route, etc. Identify all possible risks and determine what can be done to reduce or remove them. If there are neighbours nearby, you may have sound issues. To provide the authentic cinema experience you will be setting the volume of your film quite high and the sound will carry a long way. Any restrictions on sound levels or time (i.e. must be finished by 11pm) may make a film presentation outside at that location unviable.

Any additional costs incurred to address issues highlighted should be added to the quotation.

Bad Weather Contingency

You will be checking the local weather forecast regularly in the lead up to the event. Should the weather be so bad that it is unsafe to operate, or too unpleasant for the audience, you will need to have a contingency plan in place.

- is there a suitable undercover / indoor location at the venue you could use in an emergency?
- can the site be covered by hiring a marquee?
- can the event be re-arranged for another day?

Sometimes, of course, the contingency plan is 'there is no contingency' so you should always include a cancellation for bad weather clause in your written agreements.

Written Agreement

Once the site survey has been done and you are certain that all costs are known you can provide a confirmed quotation.

When the customer agrees the quote, you should send out written confirmation setting out all the details agreed and include your general terms and conditions, deposit requirements, cancellation policy and so on. If the film license has come back by this point you would include this in the agreement. If it has not, the agreement must include a clause stating the film is subject to license approval and may change.

The details of the deposit are up to you, but a non-refundable 25% on booking, with the balance payable no less than 14 days before the event, seems fair.

Ticketed Events

Much of the planning for ticketed events mirrors what you will do for private hire bookings; film selection, site survey, bad weather contingency, etc. However, there are a great deal more things to be done to prepare for your own events, not least in the promotion and sale of tickets. As you are probably not on a guaranteed income for your own event, every ticket sold adds to your bottom line.

Information Gathering

Unlike private hire events, much of the information you need to gather with come from yourself in conjunction with the venue you choose for your event.

- Nature / Theme of event.
  (i.e. summer film night, Easter, Mother's Day, valentine's day etc.)

- Venue

- Date, or selection of dates, and time convenient for you and venue

- Maximum audience capacity
  (may be constrained by size available or license)

- Film preference
  (may be date or venue specific, or just the current blockbuster)

- Ticket Price
  (usually agreed with the venue)

- Main point of contact at venue
  (technical and/or front of house)

Selecting the venue

Quirky, exciting venues will work better that standard church halls, schools and the like for indoor presentations. Why would people pay the same or more for a ticket to your popup cinema in a church hall when they could go to the local multiplex and enjoy all the comforts of a large cinema? Choose somewhere people would actually want to hang out for an evening, not just to see a movie, but to enjoy the space.

Open air, people are happy to pay more to sit outside on a blanket and picnic while watching a movie. People always look for the new and unusual, so look for historic buildings, museums, aquariums, artistic areas, small community fairs, farms, parks, areas overlooking ponds/lakes, and so on.

Bear in mind the technical requirements that need to be met when selecting your venue.

Also consider;

- promotional opportunities
    - can you put posters and flyers up around the venue and local area?
    - is the venue open to the public at other times, and will plenty of people see your posters?
    - are there staff at the venue willing to help promote the event?
    - do they have their own website and social media sites to help promote the event?
- selling tickets face to face
    - is there a visitors' centre or reception manned everyday where people can buy tickets?
    - are there staff able and willing to sell tickets for the event?
- licenses
    - do they have a Premises License that allows for public entertainment and the sale of food and alcohol (if applicable)?
    - do they have a Music License allowing the use of background music?
- catering
    - do they have onsite bar and catering?
    - will they allow third parties to sell food and drink on their premises?

- - will they allow the audience to bring their own picnic food and alcohol?
- staff
  - do they have technical staff to advise and assist with the setup (i.e. power supplies etc)?
  - will they have event staff available on the day to provide front of house, first aid and so on?
- facilities
  - do they have sufficient toilets?
  - is there sufficient car parking at or near the venue?
- environment
  - is the venue in a built-up area with neighbours close by?
  - are there any noise level or time constraints for outdoor events?

It is probable that your preferred venue will have some issues to sort out; you may need to apply for a *TEN* or Music License, for example, or arrange third parties to supply catering and so on. Generally, to begin with though, you should select venues that are well versed in putting on events, as they will have everything in place for you.

If you really want to present a film in a field in the middle of nowhere, or on a beach with no power and no shade, then it can be done. You will just need to plan ahead and arrange all the things you need yourself.

Constructing a deal with the venue

There are a number of ways in which you could construct a deal with your chosen venue. For a lot of wedding or event venues, they will see cinema evenings as a way to bring more people into their premises, giving them an opportunity to sell their goods and services and provide 'free' advertising.

Where the holy grail of deals would be for the venue to pay you a fixed fee for presenting movies at their location – and it can be done – there are a few other ways you can structure a deal.

- venue pays fixed fee for a film presentation
  - this would then be considered a private hire booking

- if the venue sells tickets, they would keep all revenue
- they would generally then be responsible for all marketing and sales costs, although you could help by promoting on your website and social media pages too
- you hire the venue for a flat fee
    - you will need to consider your earning potential and other costs
    - you will need to make sure all your technical and other requirements are met
    - you will need to determine if onsite catering is included or excluded from the hire. If excluded, can you bring third parties in to provide these?
- you hire the venue on a ticket split
    - to be negotiated, but 70 / 30 split in your favour is normal
    - marketing costs are normally shared between you and the venue
    - again, you will need to determine if onsite catering is included or excluded from the hire. If excluded, can you bring third parties in to provide these? The venue may also want a share of any income from catering or merchandise sales.
- you get free use of the venue
    - generally, the venue will then supply and keep all revenue from catering and may prohibit your audience from bring their own picnics
    - you may need to agree a percentage of any advance tickets sold on their premises or via their website and social media presence.
    - you will need to make sure all your technical and other requirements are included in the deal

Any hire agreement should be subject to site survey.

Film Selection

You should discuss film choices with your venue; they may have a better understanding of their patrons' tastes than you and can advise on the type of film that would sell best at their location. Or there may be area or seasonal specific films that suit that particular venue.

In all cases, you should agree the title with the venue prior to submitting the license application. You must ensure that the venue does not begin to promote the event themselves before you have received back the License confirmation, and that any materials they use clearly state the film classification.

Site Survey

You will have done a preliminary survey of the site when first scouting for locations, so you will probably have already checked the basics prior to selecting the venue. As before, you need;

- two dedicated power sockets no more than 50m (or maximum length of your power extension cables) from the location
- enough space to erect the screen with at least 10m air gap behind and in front in addition to being able to accommodate the audience comfortably.
- easy access to the site to set-up and strike the equipment
- facilities such as car parking and toilet

Once you have begun negotiating with the venue, a more detailed survey should be carried out, ideally with the venue's own technical and events staff on hand. You will need to agree the exact location and layout of the equipment and seating areas to provide the best possible experience for the audience. You will need to identify where tickets are to be sold and checked, entry and exit points, disabled access requirements and light sources (for exiting the area safely in the dark at the end of the performance), amongst other things. Please refer to the Event Regulations section in Chapter 2 of this guide.

Hopefully, the venue has a dedicated Events Manager in place and will have the answers to any questions you can throw at them. If not, it is up to you to establish everything and include everything you need from the venue in your hire agreement.

You must perform a risk assessment of the site, as with private event bookings, to identify and mitigate all potential risks or health and safety issues.

Determine also if there are maximum sound levels or time restrictions that must be observed.

Bad Weather Contingency

You will be checking the local weather forecast regularly in the lead up to the event. Should the weather be so bad that it is unsafe to operate, or too unpleasant for the audience, you will need to have a contingency plan in place.

- is there a suitable undercover / indoor location at the venue you could use in an emergency?
- can the site be covered by hiring a marquee?
- can the event be re-arranged for another day?

If the contingency plan is 'there is no contingency', you should always include a cancellation for bad weather clause in your hire agreement and ticket conditions of purchase.

Written Agreement

Once the site survey has been done and you are happy that everything you need to have in place has been covered you should confirm everything in writing with the venue. This agreement must clearly layout everything included in the hire, what the venue is responsible for and what you are, payment schedule and cancellation terms and conditions.

When the venue is assisting in the sale of tickets a formal accounting process needs to be agreed, detailing how and when they will update you on ticket sales, when they release money to you, how they process refunds, and so on.

Having everything down in writing avoids any arguments later.

Detailed Event Plan

If there is a dedicated event manager at your venue you should liaise regularly and have at least one formal meeting to discuss the finer details of your event. You will need to determine timings and arrangements for arriving, setting up, operating, striking and leaving site. In addition, you must decide, amongst other things;

- doors open time for the audience
- primary technical and / or event manager contact on the day
- numbers of stewards and first aiders required, and who supplies them
- any additional theming or decoration needed (for Christmas, Halloween party etc.), and who supplies them
- any additional entertainment needed (for example live music, or warm up act), and who supplies them
- audience seating arrangements (i.e. on supplied chairs, or bring their own)
- bad weather contingency

- emergency evacuation plan

Promote the event

Once the venue has been booked and the film license is confirmed you are free to begin your promotional activities, publish tickets for sale on all your sales channels, and start engaging with your audience via email, social media and printed posters and flyers.

5000 A5 Flyers and 20 A3 (or A4) posters are not too expensive and are most effective if distributed at intervals at 2 weeks, 1 week and 2 days prior to the presentation date.

Send out press releases to local media outlets and consider paid advertising and 'Groupon' discounts if ticket sales are slow.

Sell advertising space

Compile a list of potential advertisers appropriate to the location and the film being shown. Explore sponsorship options and set clear sales targets to be achieved. If you are providing graphic design services, either yourself or by outsourcing, receive approval from advertisers, and invoice for payment in full prior to the event.

Preparation

Well before the day of the event you will want to have brought all the elements together to rehearse, test and time everything. Sometimes things do go wrong on the night, but if you are well prepared and well-rehearsed, you can generally overcome anything and keep the show on the road.

Constructing the programme

Approximately one week before the event, you should bring all the elements of the programme together and run the entire event through to test for any technical issues, rehearse, and get an accurate running time for the event.

Film media

If you do not already have a copy of the film on Blu-ray, you can order it from Filmbank at the time of requesting the license, for a flat fee (currently £15). However, you will probably find the film cheaper on Amazon, or in your local video shop or supermarket. Needless to say, you should be certain that you can obtain a copy of the film prior to confirming or promoting your event.

DVD copies should be used only as a last resort, as the reduction in picture quality will be noticeable on your large cinema screen.

Background music

You will need an iTunes or Amazon account to purchase and download audio files (MP3) containing individual tracks and albums to your laptop for use as background music. If you have physical CDs, you can upload these onto your computer too.

Select music appropriate to the film being shown or event theme – there are several great soundtrack compilation albums available, which you can use over and over at your events.

Putting together a playlist of around 1 hour should be enough. Pre-show you can play this from your laptop using iTunes or Windows Media Player on random repeat to accompany any advertising being shown on screen and provide general background music as the audience arrive and take their seats. Alternatively, you can connect your MP3 or CD player and play music from there.

Compiling the advertising slideshow

Having received in all the approved advertising artwork, insert these into your slideshow template, and run the slideshow through once to test for any technical problems and to get an accurate running time.

Using the example discussed in Chapter 3, your slideshow should be 10 minutes long. You would then plan to run this on a loop 3 times to provide 30 minutes of pre-show advertising

Trailers

If you wish to show trailers for your upcoming film events you can generally find and download these from YouTube. You should only use videos marked 'Official UK trailer' as these will have received a BBFC film classification.

Only show trailers for films you have obtained licenses to show, and only those that are age appropriate for the main film you are showing. (i.e. do not run a trailer for The Rocky Horror Show that is rated 15 at a presentation of Mary Poppins 2!)

Video adverts and film shorts

If you are playing video adverts or film shorts, you should receive these in at least one week before the presentation so that you can build these into your programme.

These should all have received a BBFC film classification (unless for a private event or trade show), and you must ensure that it is appropriate for the main film you are showing.

Putting it all together

There will be up to four elements involved in the compiled programme;

- background music
  played from your laptop on a loop using iTunes (or via MP3 or CD player), commencing usually when the doors open and continuing throughout the advertising slideshow

- advertising slideshow
  run from your laptop using PowerPoint, commencing usually 30 minutes prior to main feature

- video adverts, trailers and film shorts
  run from your laptop using Windows Media Player immediately before the main feature. You will have compiled a WMP playlist with all videos to be shown in order.

- Main feature
  played from your Bluray player

Rehearse, rehearse, rehearse

At the point you begin showing the advertising slideshow (step 2 above) everything you do from then on will be 'live' and in full view of your audience on the big screen so it is really important that you develop techniques to perform the transition from one step to the next as seamlessly as possible – you do not want your audience to see you flipping between screens on your laptop, or music carrying on over the top of your trailers and main feature. You will need to mask the projector every time you transition so the screen goes dark, and you will need to fade up and down the various audio inputs.

It will take time to become proficient in this, and lots of rehearsals ahead of time will avoid too many mistakes on the night. If you do make a few mistakes however don't worry too much. Open air movie goers are a very forgiving bunch. If the atmosphere is good, and the booze is flowing, no-one will mind too much if there is an error here or there.

You can practice the transitions by rigging up your laptop and bluray player to the projector and sound system (you can project onto a blank wall so don't need to set up the screen every time).

Test everything

Prior to every event, test all equipment to ensure everything is working. Do this in enough time to allow you to resolve any technical problems before going out to the venue.

You will also need to run the film through to check the Bluray disc has no errors, and any downloaded video files to make sure there are no sound or video corruption.

If you have a credit card machine, check this is working, and can connect to your iPhone or other smart device.

The Main Event

So, you've followed your plans, prepared, rehearsed and tested in advance and now the day has arrived. The schedule of activities for the day will depend on whether it is a private booking or your own ticketed events but, the very first thing you do in either case, when you are presenting outdoors is check the latest weather report! If all is well, you can head off to the venue.

Equipment Setup and Strike

Your equipment should come with instructions on how to setup and connect it all together. You will have rehearsed this several times before your first event and will have a good idea how long it takes you to setup and check everything before your programme starts.

In general, it should take 2 people about an hour to set everything up, faster if more people are on hand to help with the screen. You should always add an extra hour on to your timings to cover any last-minute problems you may come across. Therefore, you should arrive on site no less than two hours before your 'doors open' time.

You will work most efficiently if you always setup and strike equipment in the same order, taking care to pack everything away in the same boxes and in the same location in your vehicle at the end of the day. Bear in mind that at the end of your performance light levels may be low so you should position everything as close to a light source as possible to avoid having to carry torches around or scrape around in the dark to find all the cables to pack away!

Prior to setup you should check the wind speed to ensure you are operating within the limits prescribed by the screen manufacturer.

The recommended order in which to setup (and strike) is as follows:

- screen
  it will take time to set out the frame, attach the projection surface, inflate (if applicable) and tether it to the ground in the correct location. The screen should be situated on level ground and facing the audience area head on, with an air gap of at least 10m behind (if back projecting) and in front, beyond which the audience will sit. When striking, release the tethers and lay the screen on its back prior to deflation (if applicable).

- projector
  set up the projector following the detailed instructions provided with it, and situate it on its stand at the appropriate distance in front of (or behind) the screen. The instructions will provide a guide as to the optimum distance from the screen but, you will have rehearsed this several times, during which you should have measured the distance that works best for you.

  If you are projecting from the front, you may have to situate the projector and associated equipment to one side so as not to block the view of audience directly behind you. The instructions will show you how to operate the projector, including how to align the projected image to the screen, and adjust settings to compensate for projecting at an angle.

  Please note that at time of set-up it may not be dark enough to accurately align the projector to the screen – this will have to be done once light levels are lower, possibly when your audience has already begun to arrive. To minimize the amount of alignment you need to do in front of your audience you should have pre-aligned and measured distances and angles in rehearsals and position the screen and projector as closely to that as possible. Hopefully, if you are accurate in your measurements, when it is dark enough and you switch on the projector for the first time it will be pretty well aligned to the screen anyway, so only minor tweaks will be needed to get it 100% correct.

The good news is, that so long as you always consider the site you are to work in carefully, you can always set the projector and screen up the same, so it will become second nature very quickly.

- Sound system and speakers
following the instructions provided, set up the speakers at each side of the screen and cable up to the sound system. Always follow the instructions carefully and only switch everything on in the prescribed order to avoid damage to the speakers.

- Laptop
make sure it is plugged in to the electric (you don't want to run out of battery during the pre-show!), booted up and ready to go. The video output should be plugged into the appropriate port on the projector, and the sound output into the sound system.

- Blu-ray Player
plug the HDMI video output into the appropriate port on the projector, and the stereo audio output into the sound system. Insert the Blu-ray disc so it is ready to go.

Test the sound output from both the Blu-ray player and the laptop and rehearse again how you switch between the two outputs. Set the sound levels appropriate for the event – walk around the area whilst playing sound through the speakers and decide on the optimum volume. You want to provide the authentic cinema experience to everyone, so the volume needs to be loud enough for the people furthest away to hear clearly, but not so loud as to bring the environmental officer out! You must observe any site-specific noise limitations. The sound level you chose for the background music will be lower than that of the film as when the audience are arriving they will want to be able to hear themselves talk to each other!

Once everything is set up and ready to go, and before your audience is allowed in to the area, complete any tasks highlighted as part of your risk assessment (i.e. secure and tape down all electric cables, ensure you are not blocking any emergency exits etc.). If you are setting up in a public area where there are always people moving about, you will have to do some safety work as you go along. At the very least you should put up notices to advise people that you are working in the area and task someone to keep watch for any potential risk arising.

Private Hire

How your private hire event runs, what elements you need to perform and to what schedule will be determined by the terms of your booking. You may not be required to provide background music, you will almost certainly not be running advertising and you may or may not choose to play trailers before the main feature.

If your film presentation is part of a larger event, your timings may be co-ordinated by a dedicated event planner or the customer. Be flexible, things always change at the last minute, but also always keep an eye on safety.

Even if the weather forecast is fair you will sometimes get the odd shower to deal with mid-performance. Be ready to cover the electrical equipment with ponchos or other waterproof materials, but take care not to obscure the projector lens! If you have a gazebo up over the projection desk, then you just need to get the speakers and all plug sockets covered.

At the end of the event, strike the equipment and vacate the site, leaving everything as you found out.

Ticketed Events

If you are providing or directing front of house staff make sure they are fully briefed as to what is required or them, the approximate schedule of events, and any information relating to security and facilities they need to impart to the audience.

Generate your ticket sales lists from all your ticket sales channels and provide to the box office for checking tickets on arrival. Have plenty of paper tickets available too for last minute walk-ins. Sometimes attendance can more than double on the night if it is fine weather, and you won't want to turn anyone away unless you have physically reached capacity at the venue.

Make sure all danger areas, like cable runs and screen tethers are clearly marked and cordoned off if possible. Label any plug sockets in use for the performance (you do not want someone to unplug anything by mistake during the film!)

Liaise with the venue technical and events team (if appropriate) and check everything again prior to 'opening the doors' and letting the audience in.

Once the doors are open you programme will begin.

- you will begin the background music at the appropriate sound level
- as soon as it is dark enough you can switch on and tweak the alignment of the projector
- you may then want to project a still image on the screen (your logo and website address perhaps) until it is time to begin the adverts (if any), usually 30 minutes prior to show time.

- at the end of the adverts, you will kill the background music, and play any video adverts and trailers
- you play the main feature
- at the end of the presentation run the film to the very end of the credits and if it is possible to increase light levels while the audience departs, do so.
- if it is appropriate you may decide to play exit music once the film has ended while the last few people depart, although depending on the time you may not be permitted to play anything beyond your agreed end time.
- begin striking the equipment once the audience are safely away from your work area.
- Confirm with the venue's technical or event staff when the site is clear.

Accounting

Once the evet has taken place, you will need to complete the paperwork, pay the license fee, and any other expenses you may have incurred (casual staff, 3rd party suppliers etc.)

For private hire event where no tickets were sold you will already have invoiced and received payment in full from your customer. You will need to re-confirm the details to Filmbank, who will raise an invoice for the agreed film license fee, which is payable within 7 days.

For ticketed events, including private hires where the customer paid you a flat fee, but sold tickets themselves, you will need to have a complete breakdown of ticket sales, from all sales channels as soon as possible after event, ideally by the end of the next working day.

Ticket sales may have come from multiple channels;

- your private hire customer
  in which case they must supply you with accurate figures
- your online ticket agencies (Eventbrite, WeGotTickets etc.)
  full sales reports on all ticket sites are available as soon as online ticket sales close for the event.
- advanced sales at the venue and other outlets
- on-the-door ticket sales

You must file your return with Filmbank as soon after the event as possible, ideally within 2 working days of the presentation. Filmbank will calculate the license fee due and raise an invoice for payment within 7 days.

Keep accurate, verifiable records of all sales – Filmbank reserve the right to audit your box office records at any time.

Apart from cash received on the door, you will not immediately receive income due to you;

- online ticket agencies will hold the money for 3-7 days after the event prior to releasing it to you. Payment may take a further 2-3 days to reach your bank account.
- cash taken by the venue and other advance ticket sales outlets will have to be claimed back from them.
- any balance payable by your private hire customer for the film license over and above the minimum charge already invoiced. You will need to raise an additional invoice against the customer to obtain additional funds.

You may also have income from popcorn, catering and merchandise sales, whether directly, by way of a profit share of flat fee to third parties, etc.

Profit and Loss of a Typical Event

Below is an example of a profit and loss statement which illustrates the directly attributable income and expenses for a real ticketed event.

Event description: Venue Hire Terms % of ticket sales

- open air film presentation in the grounds of a stately home on the south coast of England in September 2018.
- the venue is open to the public daily and participated in the selling of tickets on site.
- food and catering supplied by the venue with no profit share offered
- all stewards, front of house and first aid staff provided by the venue
- venue holds appropriate Premises and Music Licenses
- no advertising or other sales permitted

Comment: You will see that even without revenue from advertising sales, catering or merchandise, the net profit for one event can be well worth the effort, and serves as 'free' advertising for your popup cinema to potential private hire customers of the future.

Cash Basis

Profit Loss
Event - September 2018

	Sep 18
Ordinary Income/Expense	
Income	
Event Income	
Sales	
Box Office	
Advance Sales - DesignMyNight	160.00
Advance Sales - Eventbrite	550.00
Advance Sales - Skiddle	110.00
Advance Sales - Wegottickets	20.00
Advance Sales - Website	40.00
Cash Sales	0.00
Venue Sales	1,270.00
Total Box Office	2,150.00
Total Event	2,150.00
Total Income	2,150.00
Total Income	2,150.00
Cost of Goods Sold	
Event Cost of Goods Sold	
License Fees	
FilmBank	707.60
Total License Fees	707.60
Paypal Transaction Fees	1.56
Total Event Cost of Goods Sold	709.16
Total COGS	709.16
Gross Profit	1,440.84
Expense	
Event Expenses	
Advertising & Promotion	
Flyers / Posters	57.19
Facebook Promotions	80.72
Total Advertising & Promotion	137.91
Digital Media	
MP3 Music Files / CDs	29.89
Total Digital Media	29.89
Venue Hire	
Performance Space	645.00
Total Venue Hire	645.00
Total Event Expenses	812.80
Total Expense	812.80
Net Ordinary Income	628.04
Profit for the Year	628.04

The above excludes indirect costs that are shared across multiple events, such as insurances, motoring costs etc.

As a comparison, this is an example profit and loss for a typical private hire booking, where there are no directly attributable expenses;

Cash Basis

Profit Loss
Private Hire Booking

	One Event
Ordinary Income/Expense	
Income	
Hire Income	
Sales	
Private Hire Booking Fee	1,000.00
Total Hire	1,000.00
Total Income	1,000.00
Total Income	1,000.00
Cost of Goods Sold	
Event Cost of Goods Sold	
License Fees	
FilmBank	166.80
Total License Fees	166.80
Total Event Cost of Goods Sold	166.80
Total COGS	166.80
Gross Profit	833.20
Expense	
Event Expenses	
Total Event Expenses	0.00
Total Expense	0.00
Net Ordinary Income	833.20
Profit for the Year	833.20

Private hire bookings provide guaranteed income, without any of the associated effort or risks involved in having to promote or sell tickets or advertising space. However, your own ticketed events enable you to promote your business to a wider audience, some of whom will consider booking you for their own events in the future.

Appendix: Useful Contacts

Below you will find useful contact details for suppliers of various goods and services you may need during everyday operation of your business. This list is by no means exhaustive, and their inclusion on the list is not an endorsement. You will no doubt find your own providers as you go along, but these may help to get you started.

Suppliers – Technical

AIRSCREEN
The Airscreen Company
Hafenweg 26, 48155 Münster, Germany
+49 251 6090250
www.airscreen.com/en/

DREAM AV
0845 838 6088
129 Theobald Rd
Norwich NR1 2NY
www.dreamav.co.uk

JUST PROJECTORS
01256 882629
https://www.projectors.co.uk/
Just Projectors, 7 Campbell Court,
Bramley, Hampshire, RG26 5EG

MEDIA SERVICES LTD
(Hire Company)
0208 692 6050
Deptford Trading Estate,
Blackhorse Rd, London, SE8 5HY

PRO AUDIO CENTRE
0113 8800 138
Grunberg St
Leeds
LS6 3HH

Suppliers – Other

CUSTOM PLANET
(customised clothing, work wear)
0191 597 2670
Unit 7, Strand Business Centre
Mylord Crescent
Camperdown Ind Est
Killingworth
Newcastle Upon Tyne
NE12 5US.
www.customplanet.co.uk

GLOWTOPIA
(novelty lights and toys for resale)
01202 912 931
Unit 1 Stanley Green Industrial Estate,
Poole, Dorset, BH15 3TH
www.glowtopia.co.uk

GOODWIN GRAPHICS
(graphic design, vehicle logos)
01929 792758
Unit 2 Townsend Business Park
Bere Regis
Dorset
BH20 7LA
www.goodwingraphics.co.uk

POPCORN PLANET
(popcorn and popcorn carts, candyfloss and promotional sweets)
0800 689 5039
Unit 20, Atlas Business Centre
Oxgate Lane
London NW2 7HJ
www.popcornplanet.co.uk

ROLLER BANNERS UK
(24-hour banners and printed materials)
023 8070 0111
Unit 6, City Grove Trading Estate
Woodside Road
Eastleigh
Hampshire
SO50 4ET
www.rollerbannersuk.com

SAXOPRINT
(posters, flyers, tickets, promotional materials)
020 3608 0777
www.saxoprint.co.uk

SURF & TURF
Instant Shelters Ltd
(instant gazebos and tents)
01925 819608
Unit 7 Tatton Court, Kingsland Grange,
Warrington, Cheshire. WA1 4RR
www.surfturf.co.uk

THEME TRADERS
(Props and decorations for event themes)
020 8452 8518
Production Village, Turpins Yard,
Oaklands Road, London, NW2 6LL
www.themetraders.com

Service Providers

CASHPLUS
(online business banking)
0330 024 0925
www.cashplus.com

FILMBANK MEDIA
(film licensing)
020 7984 5957
Warner House, 98 Theobald's Road,
London, WC1X 8WB, United Kingdom
www.filmbankmedia.com

iZETTLE
(merchant account / credit card reader)
58 Victoria Embankment
London EC4Y 0DS
www.izettle.com

PPL PRS LIMITED
(music licensing)
0800 0720 808
Mercury Place
St. George's Street
Leicester
LE1 1QG
www.pplprs.co.uk

THOMAS & CO
(insurance broker)
01202 620691
23 Glenmore Business Park
Blackhill Road
Holton Heath
Poole
BH16 6NL
www.thomas-and-co.co.uk

Index

advertising, 10, 30, 32, 34, 36, 37, 38, 47, 51, 52, 53, 57, 59, 61
Amazon, 24, 51, 52
background music, 27, 42, 46, 52, 53, 56, 57, 58
bank account, 18, 29, 59
Bluray, 22, 23, 24, 53, 54, 56
book-keeping, 18
box office receipts, 24
cancellation policy, 33, 45
cancellations, 33
Cashplus, 18
copyright, 36
credit card, 18, 31, 54
distributors, 23, 24
dry hire, 10, 19
Eventbrite, 29, 30, 33, 58
Facebook, 30, 34
film classification, 22, 49, 52, 53
film shorts, 39, 53
Filmbank, 23, 24, 36
FilmBank, 43, 51, 58, 59
first aid, 27, 47, 59
Flyers, 35
food safety, 27
future growth, 9
Health and Safety at Work, 26
HMRC, 17, 18, 19
initial assets, 10
Instagram, 30
insurance, 10, 19, 28
iTunes, 52, 53
iZettle, 18
Laptop, 56

license, 9, 22, 23, 24, 25, 26, 36, 40, 42, 43, 45, 48, 51, 58, 59
licensing, 9, 21, 29
Limited company, 17
Limited Company, 17, 19
Microsoft Powerpoint, 39
Mystery shoppers, 22
noise control, 27
original poster artwork, 36
playlist, 39, 52, 53
policies, 19, 31, 33
popcorn, 10, 18, 40, 42, 59
Posters, 35
PPL, 25
private hire, 9, 21, 22, 23, 24, 34, 37, 38, 41, 45, 47, 56, 58, 59, 61
Private hire, 9, 41, 61
Private Hire, 35, 41, 56
profit and loss, 59, 61
projector, 42, 44, 53, 54, 55, 56, 57
PRS, 25
public entertainments, 25
public liability, 19, 28
Quickbooks, 19
refunds, 33, 50
regulations, 26, 36
risk assessment, 26, 44, 49, 56
Saxoprint, 35
screen, 19, 23, 27, 34, 37, 42, 43, 44, 49, 52, 53, 54, 55, 56, 57
security, 27, 57
self-employed, 17, 18, 19

selling tickets, 22, 23, 24, 32, 35, 36, 46
slideshow, 37, 39, 52, 53
social media, 30, 34, 46, 48, 51
sole trader, 17, 18
Sole Trader, 17
Sound system, 56
speakers, 11, 56, 57
stewards, 27, 50, 59
Subscribe to Newsletter, 36
tax returns, 18, 19
Temporary Events Notice, 23, 25
TheMusicLicens e, 25
third party suppliers, 10
ticket sales, 9, 22, 30, 31, 32, 33, 37, 50, 51, 57, 58, 59
ticketed, 9, 21, 24, 29, 34, 41, 45, 54, 58, 59, 61
Ticketed Events, 41, 45, 57
trailers, 21, 22, 37, 39, 52, 53, 57, 58
Twitter, 30
VAT, 17, 18, 24, 29
venue, 9, 10, 22, 23, 24, 25, 26, 29, 32, 33, 35, 40, 42, 44, 45, 46, 47, 48, 49, 50, 51, 54, 57, 58, 59
video adverts, 39, 53, 58
weather, 26, 34, 44, 45, 49, 50, 54, 57
website, 18, 19, 22, 24, 25, 29, 30, 31, 35, 36, 46, 48, 57
wind speed, 15, 19, 27, 34, 55
Window Media Player, 39

www.ingramcontent.com/pod-product-compliance
Lightning Source LLC
Chambersburg PA
CBHW060438220526
45465CB00008B/3191